To Geoff, Leslie, David, and Declan—once neighbors, friends always —M.S.
For Mac, Mima, and Fox —R.A.

A special thank you to Kelsea Jacobsen, education program manager for the Compost Research & Education Foundation, for sharing your composting expertise.

Printed in China
First Edition

For information about special discounts for bulk purchases, please contact W. W. Norton Special Sales at specialsales@wwnorton.com or 800-233-4830

Manufacturing by Toppan Leefung
Book design by Rilla Alexander and Hana Anouk Nakamura
Production manager: Delaney Adams

ISBN 978-1-324-08308-5

Library of Congress Cataloging-in-Publication Data

Names: Schaub, Michelle author | Alexander, Rilla illustrator

Title: Pumpkin smash / Michelle Schaub ; illustrated by Rilla Alexander.

Description: First edition. | New York : Norton Young Readers, [2026] | Audience: Ages 4–6 | Audience: Grades K–1 | Summary: Instead of the trash, give pumpkins a smash, and watch them feed the soil in a composting bash!

Identifiers: LCCN 2026003971 | ISBN 9781324083085 hardcover

Subjects: CYAC: Stories in rhyme | Jack-o-lanterns—Fiction | Pumpkins—Fiction | Compost—Fiction | LCGFT: Stories in rhyme | Picture books | Fiction

Classification: LCC PZ8.3.S2971225 Pu 2026 | DDC [E]—dc23/eng/2025
LC record available at https://lccn.loc.gov/2026003971

W. W. Norton & Company, Inc., 500 Fifth Avenue, New York, NY 10110
www.wwnorton.com

W. W. Norton & Company Ltd., 15 Carlisle Street, London W1D 3BS

Authorized EU representative: EAS, Mustamäe tee 50, 10621 Tallinn, Estonia

1 2 3 4 5 6 7 8 9 0

Michelle Schaub

Illustrated by
Rilla Alexander

PUMPKIN SMASH!

Norton Young Readers
An Imprint of W. W. Norton & Company
Independent Publishers Since 1923

On Halloween night,
jack-o'-lanterns shine bright.

With jagged grins
and gleaming eyes,
from windows
and porches
and stairs,
they spy.

What a delightful,
frightful
sight!

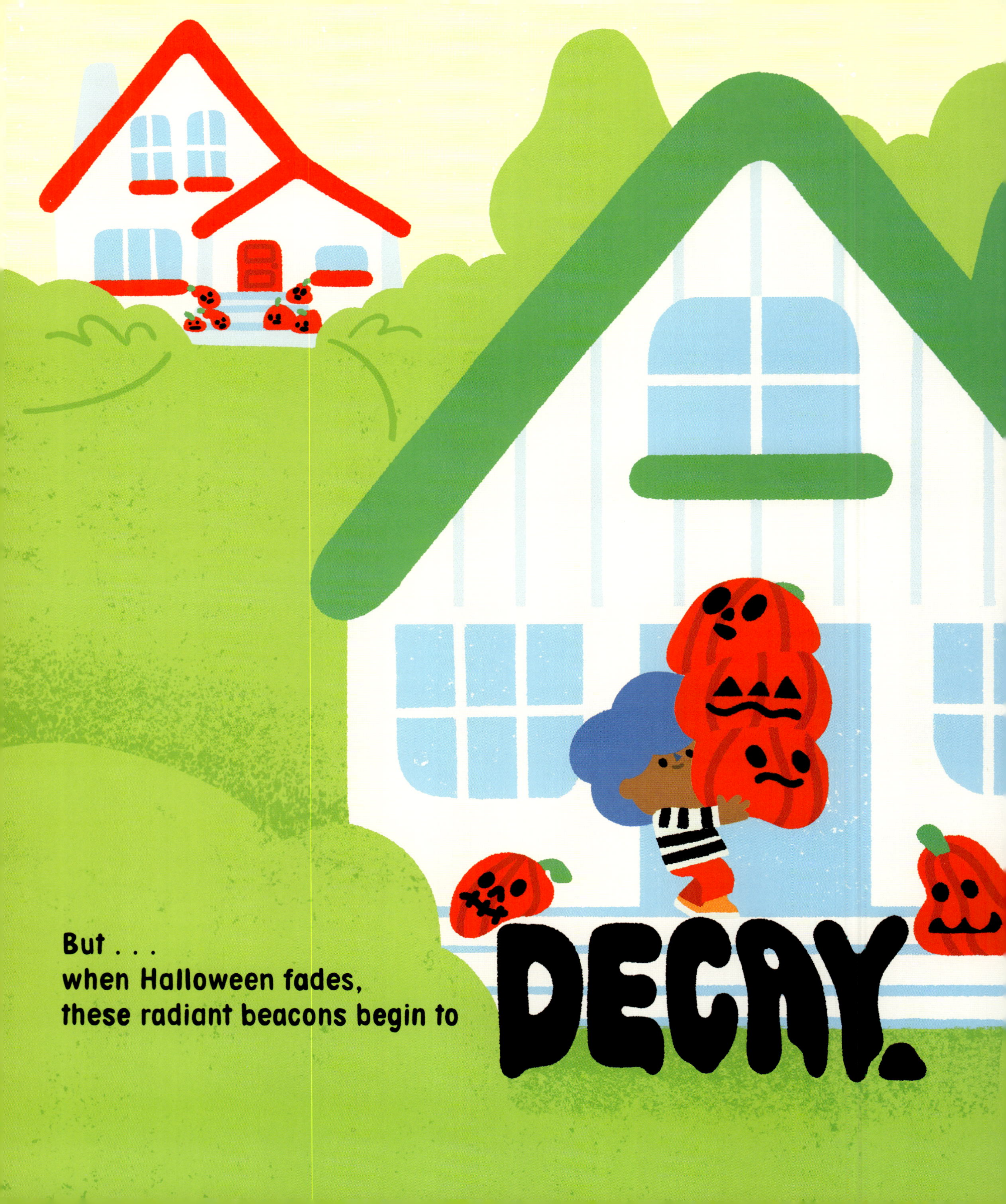

But . . .
when Halloween fades,
these radiant beacons begin to

DECAY.

They slouch on their stoops.
Their smiles start to droop.
Their insides dissolve
into foul, moldy goop.

Time to throw
those pumpkins away.

But, WAIT!

Moldy pumpkins tossed with trash
fill our landfills,
where they pass
loads of vile
and
stinky
gas.

PEE-EW!

What's a pumpkin fan to do?

Instead of dumping
rotting pumpkins,
take them to a . . .

What's that?

A place to gather sagging pumpkins
(worn-out gourds are welcome, too!)
and squish those squash
to pulpy bits
to mix into a compost brew.

Time to choose
your smashing tool!

Will you use a baseball bat?

Tee it up and take a swing!

Just . . . like . . . that.

Maybe launch it from a sling?

Jack-o'-lanterns on the wing!

Or climb up high
and let it drop.

Turn it into
pumpkin slop.

Or wear a pair
of muck-proof boots
and stomp all over spoiling fruits.

Jump and leap!
Skip and prance!

Do a sloshy-squashy dance!

Stringy lumps
and slimy clumps.
Mushy, gushy
pumpkin gunk.

All those chunks
beneath your toes
are ready now to . . .

DECOM

POSE!

In compost heaps,
they'll snuggle deep,
with leaves and grass,
and kitchen scraps,
slowly turning,
over time . . .

. . . from cast-off
spoils
to FOOD
for soil.

In spring,
when nourished earth is rich,
dig a hole
and plant a seed.

Watch your pumpkin
s l o w l y

grow.

When it's ready,
carve a grin,
and add two bright
and shining eyes.

Let it light
All Hallows' Night.

Then, when Halloween has passed,
you'll know what to do . . .

SH!

An Abundance of Pumpkins

More than one billion pounds of pumpkins are grown in the United States each year. Many pumpkins are carved into brightly shining jack-o'-lanterns. But when Halloween is over, millions of sagging pumpkins and worn-out gourds are tossed in the trash. These cast-off squashes end up in landfills.

Pumpkins at the Dump? Pee-ew!

Landfills are designed to store material, not allow it to decompose. When everything is compacted in a landfill, the materials inside don't have access to oxygen. Without oxygen, organic matter like pumpkins produces methane, a smelly gas that contributes to our warming climate. In addition, pumpkins are 90 percent water. All that water can seep through a landfill, mixing with dangerous chemicals which then leak into our groundwater.

Don't Trash 'em, Smash 'em!

To keep jack-o'-lanterns from clogging landfills, many communities sponsor post-Halloween PUMPKIN SMASHES. A pumpkin smash is a recycling round-up where pumpkins and gourds past their prime are prepared for composting. These events often feature fun activities like launching pumpkins from slingshots or tossing them at targets. The goal is to break the pumpkins down into small pieces. Those small chunks decompose faster and can be composted.

From Scraps to Soil

Composting is a method of recycling organic matter. In a compost pile, organic materials like pumpkin chunks are broken down by bacteria, fungi, and other decomposers into fine particles. These particles are the basis for a healthy soil food web. When added to soil, compost can improve plant health, better store water and nutrients, and help reduce erosion and water pollution.

Check with your local municipality to find a post-Halloween pumpkin smash near you.

Want to try your hand at home composting? Learn more at https://www.epa.gov/recycle/composting-home

Composting pumpkins is a great way to reduce landfill waste, protect waterways, and make the soil rich and healthy . . . so you can grow MORE PUMPKINS!